THIS BOOK BELONGS TO

_____

START DATE

_____

SHE READS TRUTH

EXECUTIVE

FOUNDER/CHIEF EXECUTIVE OFFICER
Raechel Myers

CO-FOUNDER/CHIEF CONTENT OFFICER
Amanda Bible Williams

CHIEF OPERATING OFFICER
Ryan Myers

EXECUTIVE ASSISTANT
Sarah Andereck

EDITORIAL

CONTENT DIRECTOR
John Greco, MDiv

MANAGING EDITOR
Jessica Lamb

CONTENT EDITOR
Kara Gause

ASSOCIATE EDITORS
Bailey Gillespie
Ellen Taylor

CREATIVE

CREATIVE DIRECTOR
Jeremy Mitchell

LEAD DESIGNER
Kelsea Allen

DESIGNERS
Abbey Benson
Davis DeLisi
Annie Glover

MARKETING

MARKETING DIRECTOR
Hannah Warren

MARKETING MANAGER
Katie Pierce

SOCIAL MEDIA MANAGER
Ansley Rushing

COMMUNITY SUPPORT SPECIALIST
Margot Williams

SHIPPING & LOGISTICS

LOGISTICS MANAGER
Lauren Gloyne

SHIPPING MANAGER
Sydney Bess

CUSTOMER SUPPORT SPECIALIST
Katy McKnight

FULFILLMENT SPECIALISTS
Abigail Achord
Cait Baggerman
Kamiren Passavanti

SUBSCRIPTION INQUIRIES
orders@shereadstruth.com

CONTRIBUTORS

RECIPE
Beth Matuska (40)

PHOTOGRAPHER
Katie Wilson (Cover, 57, 89)

@SHEREADSTRUTH

Download the
She Reads Truth app,
available for iOS
and Android

Subscribe to the
She Reads Truth podcast

SHEREADSTRUTH.COM

SHE READS TRUTH™

© 2020 by She Reads Truth, LLC

All rights reserved.

All photography used by permission.

ISBN 978-1-949526-94-3

1 2 3 4 5 6 7 8 9 10

All Scripture is taken from the Christian Standard Bible®. Copyright © 2017 by Holman Bible Publishers. Used by permission. Christian Standard Bible® and CSB® are federally registered trademarks of Holman Bible Publishers.

Research support provided by Logos Bible Software™. Learn more at logos.com.

Though the dates in this book have been carefully researched, scholars disagree on the dating of many biblical events.

This book was printed offset in Nashville, Tennessee, on 70# Lynx Opaque. Cover is 100# Cougar Opaque with a soft touch lamination.

EPHESIANS

Praise God for the wild, enduring miracle that is the Body of Christ.

Jessica

Jessica Lamb
MANAGING EDITOR

When my parents moved our family to Texas in the early '90s, we joined a large church in our new town. We found our place at a contemporary Sunday service, where worship lyrics were projected onto walls and the pastor swapped his wooden pulpit for a music stand. After service, I'd run around back corridors of the auditorium with friends, playing hide-and-seek in racks of white baptismal robes.

We often made weekend trips back to our native Arkansas, where our presence on Sundays at my grandparents' small church was always warmly noticed. We'd slide down the same pew my grandparents had held since the 1970s, and I practiced my reading skills in the order of service, asking my grandmother in loud whispers what words like *invocation* and *kyrie* meant.

Now, my husband and I meet with our church in a middle school gym. Our four-year-old daughter delights in seeing the yellow school buses lined up outside every Sunday morning, almost as much as she enjoys refusing to high-five the greeters as she enters the building.

The list of differences between these churches isn't short, spanning from order of service to how attendees dress, from views on baptism to how internal debates about new carpet were resolved. Still, when I think about these church families—their love for Jesus and one another—I stop what I'm doing to thank God for them (Eph 1:15–16).

As Paul constantly reminds his readers, our shared faith is more essential than our differences. The church at Ephesus needed this reminder to focus on what they held in common, both as a local community and as believers who shared the same faith as the broader Church in places like Galatia, Philippi, Rome, and beyond. Part of the miracle of our faith is that two thousand years later, we're part of this same family. Our brothers and sisters are sitting next to us on Sunday mornings, they are reading the Word across our towns and around the world, and they were listening to Paul's letter at a house in Ephesus in the early AD 60s. We are united in Christ.

This theme of unity is woven throughout Ephesians, so we've included weekly questions as well as a prompt on page 16 to help you to take note of it. You'll find a map on page 54 of some of the other churches Paul planted and strengthened in the gospel, all different but one in Jesus. And look for the shortbread cookie recipe on page 40—it was intentionally created to pair with the chai tea recipe in our Galatians Study Book!

As believers, we've been adopted into God's family and raised to new life with Jesus. Praise God for the wild, enduring miracle that is the Body of Christ.

DESIGN ON PURPOSE

At She Reads Truth, we believe in pairing the inherently beautiful Word of God with the aesthetic beauty it deserves. Each of our resources is thoughtfully and artfully designed to highlight the beauty, goodness, and truth of Scripture in a way that reflects the themes of each curated reading plan.

Third in our series on Paul's epistles, this book continues to highlight the terrazzo pattern that appears in our Galatians (2019) and Philippians (2020) Study Books. The cement texture infused with marble, granite, quartz, and glass chips reminds us of a key theme in Ephesians: the diverse Body of Christ is united by the same Spirit, whether we are together or apart.

HOW TO USE THIS BOOK

She Reads Truth is a community of women dedicated to reading the Word of God every day.

The Bible is living and active, breathed out by God, and we confidently hold it higher than anything we can do or say. This book focuses primarily on Scripture, with bonus resources to facilitate deeper engagement with God's Word.

SCRIPTURE READING

Designed for a Monday start, this Study Book presents the book of Ephesians in daily readings, with supplemental passages for additional context.

JOURNALING SPACE

Each weekday features space for personal reflection and prayer.

GRACE DAY

Use Saturdays to catch up on your reading, pray, and rest in the presence of the Lord.

WEEKLY TRUTH

Sundays are set aside for Scripture memorization.

EXTRAS

This book features additional tools to help you gain a deeper understanding of the text.

Devotionals corresponding to each daily reading can be found in the **Ephesians** reading plan at SheReadsTruth.com or on the She Reads Truth app. We invite you to join women from Albuquerque to Argentina in conversation and community as you read along.

CONTENTS

The book of Ephesians is a letter, originally intended to be read all at once. Find the insert in your book and take some time before you begin day 1 to read Ephesians in one sitting.

For you are saved by grace through faith, and this is not from yourselves; it is God's gift—not from works, so that no one can boast.

☙ KEY VERSE EPHESIANS 2:8–9

ON THE TIMELINE

A LITTLE BACKGROUND

Paul, the clearly identified author of Ephesians (Eph 1:1), wrote the letter while in prison (Eph 3:1; 4:1; 6:20). There is disagreement concerning whether he was imprisoned in Caesarea (Ac 24:22) or Rome (Ac 28:30) at the time, but tradition suggests Paul wrote the letter from Rome around AD 60–61. This would have been while Paul was under house arrest awaiting his appeal before Caesar (Ac 28:23–31). Paul most likely wrote Philippians, Colossians, and Philemon during the same imprisonment.

Relatively little is known about the recipients of this letter. In fact, some important early manuscripts do not contain the words "at Ephesus" (Eph 1:1). The letter was carried to its destination by Tychicus, who is identified in Ephesians 6:21 and Colossians 4:7 as Paul's messenger. Since Paul noted in both letters that Tychius would inform the churches of Paul's situation, we can assume the letters to the Ephesians and the Colossians were delivered at the same time.

MESSAGE & PURPOSE

GIVE THANKS FOR THE BOOK OF EPHESIANS

The overall theme of Ephesians is the unity of the Church in Christ through the power of the Spirit. The doctrine of the new creation corrects the misguided view that God accepts the Jew and rejects the Gentile. Paul taught that this distinction was abolished at Christ's sacrificial death, and no barrier remains to reuniting all humanity as the people of God, with Christ as the head (Eph 1:22–23). The new Body, the Church, has been endowed with the power of the Holy Spirit to enable the members to live out their new lives (Eph 1:3–2:10) and put Christ's standards into practice (Eph 4:1–6:9).

Paul's letter to the Ephesians is an anthem to the sovereign grace of God displayed toward sinners in Christ. It contains some of the worst news ("you were dead in your trespasses and sins," Eph 2:1) and best news ("But God... made us alive with Christ," Eph 2:4–5) in all of Scripture. In view of this grace, Paul calls believers to "live worthy of the calling" (Eph 4:1) we have received.

How to Read a New Testament Letter

Most of the books that make up the New Testament are letters. These letters, also called *epistles*, come in a variety of shapes and sizes. Many are considered lengthy by ancient standards. Some were addressed to churches, while others were written to individuals. Some have been passed down to us with a name borrowed from their recipients, while others are known by their author.

HERE ARE SOME PRINCIPLES TO KEEP IN MIND AS YOU READ EPHESIANS AND OTHER NEW TESTAMENT LETTERS.

READING A LETTER CAN BE LIKE LISTENING TO ONE SIDE OF A CONVERSATION.

Because we don't always know what specific questions or situations a writer was addressing, we must look for clues in what was written to figure out what was going on.

LETTERS WERE MEANT TO BE READ ALL AT ONCE.

While there's nothing wrong with studying a particular passage or even a single verse, ancient letters, like the letters we write today, were meant to be read in a single sitting. Doing so allows the reader to see the author's progression of thought and make connections that might otherwise be missed.

THE NEW TESTAMENT LETTERS WERE WRITTEN TO BELIEVERS LEARNING TO LIVE IN CHRISTIAN COMMUNITY.

With a few exceptions (1 & 2 Timothy, Titus, Philemon, and 3 John), the letters in the New Testament were written to churches—groups of people who were learning to live as the people of God. When you see "you" in these letters, it's usually plural. These letters were typically read out loud so all could hear. They were even shared between congregations (Col 4:16).

| INSTRUCTIONS WERE OFTEN TAILORED FOR A SPECIFIC AUDIENCE. | (4) | Not every instruction is meant to be applied by readers today. Some bits of guidance were written to counter a specific problem or abuse, while others articulate principles that are universally true. |

INSTRUCTIONS WERE OFTEN TAILORED FOR A SPECIFIC AUDIENCE.

(4) Not every instruction is meant to be applied by readers today. Some bits of guidance were written to counter a specific problem or abuse, while others articulate principles that are universally true.

NEW TESTAMENT LETTERS DRAW HEAVILY ON THE OLD TESTAMENT.

(5) The Old Testament was the Bible of the early Church. Because it is "profitable for teaching, for rebuking, for correcting, [and] for training in righteousness" (2Tm 3:16), it was rightly applied to situations of all kinds. The better we know the Old Testament, the better equipped we will be to understand the New Testament letters.

THE NEW TESTAMENT LETTERS WERE ALL WRITTEN TO PEOPLE LEARNING TO FOLLOW CHRIST.

(6) Whether Jewish or Gentile believers, the recipients of the New Testament letters had been rescued from the kingdom of darkness (Col 1:13). Nearly everything they thought they knew about the world and their place in it changed as a result of their entrance into God's kingdom. This new life came with its share of spiritual attacks, persecution, and mistakes. We read these letters today as fellow citizens who also have room to grow.

THE NEW TESTAMENT LETTERS ARE PART OF OUR FAMILY HISTORY.

(7) These letters make up some of the earliest records we have of the Church. Much has changed in the last two thousand years, but the faith that brought hope to Christians in the Greco-Roman world is the same faith we hold on to today. Despite differences in culture, education, and language, we have much in common with the original recipients of the New Testament letters, namely the love of Jesus Christ.

JESUS IS THE POINT.

(8) Though the New Testament letters were written years after Jesus's life, death, and resurrection, each and every one is about Him. These documents were penned so that readers would grow in their understanding of who He is, what He has done and has promised to do, and as a result become more like Him.

Unity in Ephesians

Unity in Christ is one of the key themes in the book of Ephesians. Paul encourages all believers to remember they are living together as brothers and sisters in Christ, united by the same Spirit in collective service, submission, and worship (Eph 4:3).

As you read through the book of Ephesians over the next three weeks, keep the theme of unity in mind. Underline or highlight this topic as it appears in your daily reading.

What Does the Bible Say About Unity?

How good and pleasant it is
when brothers live together in harmony!

PSALM 133:1

"But you are not to be called 'Rabbi,' because you have one Teacher, and you are all brothers and sisters."

MATTHEW 23:8

Now the entire group of those who believed were of one heart and mind, and no one claimed that any of his possessions was his own, but instead they held everything in common. With great power the apostles were giving testimony to the resurrection of the Lord Jesus, and great grace was on all of them. For there was not a needy person among them because all those who owned lands or houses sold them, brought the proceeds of what was sold, and laid them at the apostles' feet. This was then distributed to each person as any had need.

ACTS 4:32–35

Rejoice with those who rejoice; weep with those who weep. Live in harmony with one another. Do not be proud; instead, associate with the humble. Do not be wise in your own estimation.

ROMANS 12:15–16

Now I urge you, brothers and sisters, in the name of our Lord Jesus Christ, that all of you agree in what you say, that there be no divisions among you, and that you be united with the same understanding and the same conviction.

1 CORINTHIANS 1:10

Therefore I, the prisoner in the Lord, urge you to live worthy of the calling you have received, with all humility and gentleness, with patience, bearing with one another in love, making every effort to keep the unity of the Spirit through the bond of peace. There is one body and one Spirit—just as you were called to one hope at your calling—one Lord, one faith, one baptism, one God and Father of all, who is above all and through all and in all.

EPHESIANS 4:1–6

01 God's Rich Blessings

Ephesians 1:1–14

GREETING

[1] Paul, an apostle of Christ Jesus by God's will:

To the faithful saints in Christ Jesus at Ephesus.

[2] Grace to you and peace from God our Father and the Lord Jesus Christ.

GOD'S RICH BLESSINGS

[3] Blessed is the God and Father of our Lord Jesus Christ, who has blessed us with every spiritual blessing in the heavens in Christ. [4] For he chose us in him, before the foundation of the world, to be holy and blameless in love before him. [5] He predestined us to be adopted as sons through Jesus Christ for himself, according to the good pleasure of his will, [6] to the praise of his glorious grace that he lavished on us in the Beloved One.

[7] In him we have redemption through his blood, the forgiveness of our trespasses, according to the riches of his grace [8] that he richly poured out on us with all wisdom and understanding. [9] He made known to us the

mystery of his will, according to his good pleasure that he purposed in Christ [10] as a plan for the right time—to bring everything together in Christ, both things in heaven and things on earth in him.

[11] In him we have also received an inheritance, because we were predestined according to the plan of the one who works out everything in agreement with the purpose of his will, [12] so that we who had already put our hope in Christ might bring praise to his glory.

[13] In him you also were sealed with the promised Holy Spirit when you heard the word of truth, the gospel of your salvation, and when you believed. [14] The Holy Spirit is the down payment of our inheritance, until the redemption of the possession, to the praise of his glory.

John 1:12–13

[12] But to all who did receive him, he gave them the right to be children of God,

to those who believe in his name, [13] who were born, not of natural descent, or of the will of the flesh, or of the will of man, but of God.

1 Peter 1:18–21

[18] For you know that you were redeemed from your empty way of life inherited from your fathers, not with perishable things like silver or gold, [19] but with the precious blood of Christ, like that of an unblemished and spotless lamb. [20] He was foreknown before the foundation of the world but was revealed in these last times for you. [21] Through him you believe in God, who raised him from the dead and gave him glory, so that your faith and hope are in God.

notes

I pray that the eyes of your
heart may be enlightened.

EPHESIANS 1:18

02 Prayer for Spiritual Insight

WEEK 1

Ephesians 1:15–19

PRAYER FOR SPIRITUAL INSIGHT

WEEK 2

WEEK 3

[15] This is why, since I heard about your faith in the Lord Jesus and your love for all the saints, [16] I never stop giving thanks for you as I remember you in my prayers. [17] I pray that the God of our Lord Jesus Christ, the glorious Father, would give you the Spirit of wisdom and revelation in the knowledge of him. [18] I pray that the eyes of your heart may be enlightened so that you may know what is the hope of his calling, what is the wealth of his glorious inheritance in the saints, [19] and what is the immeasurable greatness of his power toward us who believe, according to the mighty working of his strength.

Proverbs 2:1–11

[1] My son, if you accept my words
and store up my commands within you,
[2] listening closely to wisdom
and directing your heart to understanding;
[3] furthermore, if you call out to insight
and lift your voice to understanding,
[4] if you seek it like silver
and search for it like hidden treasure,
[5] then you will understand the fear of the LORD
and discover the knowledge of God.
[6] For the LORD gives wisdom;
from his mouth come knowledge and understanding.
[7] He stores up success for the upright;
He is a shield for those who live with integrity
[8] so that he may guard the paths of justice
and protect the way of his faithful followers.
[9] Then you will understand righteousness, justice,
and integrity—every good path.
[10] For wisdom will enter your heart,
and knowledge will delight you.
[11] Discretion will watch over you,
and understanding will guard you.

Romans 8:18–27

[18] For I consider that the sufferings of this present time are not worth comparing with the glory that is going to be revealed to us. [19] For the creation eagerly waits with anticipation for God's sons to be revealed. [20] For the creation was subjected to futility—not willingly, but because of him who subjected it—in the hope [21] that the creation itself will also be set free from the bondage to decay into the glorious freedom of God's children. [22] For we know that the whole creation has been groaning together with labor pains until now. [23] Not only that, but we ourselves who have the Spirit as the firstfruits—we also groan within ourselves, eagerly waiting for adoption, the redemption of our bodies. [24] Now in this hope we were saved, but hope that is seen is not hope, because who hopes for what he sees? [25] Now if we hope for what we do not see, we eagerly wait for it with patience.

[26] In the same way the Spirit also helps us in our weakness,

because we do not know what to pray for as we should, but the Spirit himself intercedes for us, all with unspoken groanings. [27] And he who searches our hearts knows the mind of the Spirit, because he intercedes for the saints according to the will of God.

notes

03 # God's Power in Christ

WEEK 1

WEEK 2

WEEK 3

Ephesians 1:20–23

GOD'S POWER IN CHRIST

[20] He exercised this power in Christ by raising him from the dead and seating him at his right hand in the heavens— [21] far above every ruler and authority, power and dominion, and every title given, not only in this age but also in the one to come. [22] And he subjected everything under his feet and appointed him as head over everything for the church, [23] which is his body, the fullness of the one who fills all things in every way.

Psalm 8

For the choir director: on the Gittith. A psalm of David.

¹ LORD, our Lord,
how magnificent is your name throughout the earth!
You have covered the heavens with your majesty.
² From the mouths of infants and nursing babies,
you have established a stronghold
on account of your adversaries
in order to silence the enemy and the avenger.

³ When I observe your heavens,
the work of your fingers,
the moon and the stars,
which you set in place,
⁴ what is a human being that you remember him,
a son of man that you look after him?
⁵ You made him little less than God
and crowned him with glory and honor.
⁶ You made him ruler over the works of your hands;
you put everything under his feet:
⁷ all the sheep and oxen,
as well as the animals in the wild,
⁸ the birds of the sky,
and the fish of the sea
that pass through the currents of the seas.

⁹ LORD, our Lord,
how magnificent is your name throughout the earth!

Isaiah 11:1–9

¹ Then a shoot will grow from the stump of Jesse,
and a branch from his roots will bear fruit.
² The Spirit of the LORD will rest on him—
a Spirit of wisdom and understanding,
a Spirit of counsel and strength,
a Spirit of knowledge and of the fear of the LORD.
³ His delight will be in the fear of the LORD.

He will not judge
by what he sees with his eyes,
he will not execute justice
by what he hears with his ears,
[4] but he will judge the poor righteously
and execute justice for the oppressed of the land.
He will strike the land
with a scepter from his mouth,
and he will kill the wicked
with a command from his lips.
[5] Righteousness will be a belt around his hips;
faithfulness will be a belt around his waist.

[6] The wolf will dwell with the lamb,
and the leopard will lie down with the goat.
The calf, the young lion, and the fattened calf will be together,
and a child will lead them.
[7] The cow and the bear will graze,
their young ones will lie down together,
and the lion will eat straw like cattle.
[8] An infant will play beside the cobra's pit,
and a toddler will put his hand into a snake's den.

[9] They will not harm or
destroy each other
on my entire holy mountain,
for the land will be as full
of the knowledge of the LORD
as the sea is filled with water.

noTes

04 From Death to Life

WEEK 1

WEEK 2

WEEK 3

Ephesians 2:1–10

FROM DEATH TO LIFE

[1] And you were dead in your trespasses and sins [2] in which you previously lived according to the ways of this world, according to the ruler of the power of the air, the spirit now working in the disobedient. [3] We too all previously lived among them in our fleshly desires, carrying out the inclinations of our flesh and thoughts, and we were by nature children under wrath as the others were also. [4] But God, who is rich in mercy, because of his great love that he had for us, [5] made us alive with Christ even though we were dead in trespasses. You are saved by grace! [6] He also raised us up with him and seated us with him in the heavens in Christ Jesus, [7] so that in the coming ages he might display the immeasurable riches of his grace through his kindness to us in Christ Jesus. [8] For you are saved by grace through faith, and this is not from yourselves; it is God's gift— [9] not from works, so that no one can boast. [10] For we are his workmanship, created in Christ Jesus for good works, which God prepared ahead of time for us to do.

John 3:16–21

[16] "For God loved the world in this way: He gave his one and only Son, so that everyone who believes in him will not perish but have eternal life. [17] For God did not send his Son into the world to condemn the world, but to save the world through him. [18] Anyone who believes in him is not condemned, but anyone who does not believe is already condemned, because he has not believed in the name of the one and only Son of God. [19] This is the judgment: The light has come into the world, and people loved darkness rather than the light because their deeds were evil. [20] For everyone who does evil hates the light and avoids it, so that his deeds may not be exposed. [21] But anyone who lives by the truth comes to the light, so that his works may be shown to be accomplished by God."

1 John 5:1–13

[1] Everyone who believes that Jesus is the Christ has been born of God, and everyone who loves the Father also loves the one born of him. [2] This is how we know that we love God's children: when we love God and obey his commands. [3] For this is what love for God is: to keep his commands. And his commands are not a burden, [4] because everyone who has been born of God conquers the world. This is the victory that has conquered the world: our faith.

THE CERTAINTY OF GOD'S TESTIMONY

[5] Who is the one who conquers the world but the one who believes that Jesus is the Son of God? [6] Jesus Christ—he is the one who came by water and blood, not by water only, but by water and by blood. And the Spirit is the one who testifies, because the Spirit is the truth. [7] For there are three that testify: [8] the Spirit, the water, and the blood—and these three are in agreement. [9] If we accept human testimony, God's testimony is greater, because it is God's testimony that he has given about his Son. [10] The one who believes in the Son of God has this testimony within himself. The one who does not believe God has made him a liar, because he has not believed in the testimony God has given about his Son. [11] And this is the testimony: God has given us eternal life, and this life is in his Son. [12] The one who has the Son has life. The one who does not have the Son of God does not have life. [13] I have written these things to you who believe in the name of the Son of God so that you may know that you have eternal life.

notes

From Death to Life

Scripture speaks of salvation as a transformation—a rebirth or coming to life. Ephesians 2 illustrates the nature of this transformation in a series of comparisons between what we were before coming to faith and what we become after.

Old Life

EPHESIANS 2:1–3

WE WERE DEAD.

WE WERE ENSLAVED.

EPHESIANS 2:4–6

WE ARE ALIVE.

WE ARE ENTHRONED.

New Life

WE WERE OBJECTS OF WRATH.

WE WALKED AMONG THE DISOBEDIENT.

WE WERE UNDER SATAN'S DOMINION.

WE ARE OBJECTS OF GRACE.

WE FELLOWSHIP WITH CHRIST.

WE ARE UNIFIED WITH CHRIST.

05 Unity in Christ

WEEK 1

WEEK 2

WEEK 3

Ephesians 2:11–22

UNITY IN CHRIST

[11] So then, remember that at one time you were Gentiles in the flesh—called "the uncircumcised" by those called "the circumcised," which is done in the flesh by human hands. [12] At that time you were without Christ, excluded from the citizenship of Israel, and foreigners to the covenants of promise, without hope and without God in the world. [13] But now in Christ Jesus, you who were far away have been brought near by the blood of Christ. [14] For he is our peace, who made both groups one and tore down the dividing wall of hostility. In his flesh, [15] he made of no effect the law consisting of commands and expressed in regulations, so that he might create in himself one new man from the two, resulting in peace. [16] He did this so that he might reconcile both to God in one body through the cross by which he put the hostility to death. [17] He came and proclaimed the good news of peace to you who were far away and peace to those who were near. [18] For through him we both have access in one Spirit to the Father.

[19] So then you are no longer foreigners and strangers, but fellow citizens with the saints, and members of God's household, [20] built on the foundation of the apostles and prophets, with Christ Jesus himself as the cornerstone. [21] In him the whole building, being put together, grows into a holy temple in the Lord. [22] In him you are also being built together for God's dwelling in the Spirit.

Psalm 118:22

The stone that the builders rejected
has become the cornerstone.

Romans 12:1–8

A LIVING SACRIFICE

[1] Therefore, brothers and sisters, in view of the mercies of God, I urge you to present your bodies as a living sacrifice, holy and pleasing to God; this is your true worship. [2] Do not be conformed to this age, but be transformed by the renewing of your mind, so that you may discern what is the good, pleasing, and perfect will of God.

MANY GIFTS BUT ONE BODY

[3] For by the grace given to me, I tell everyone among you not to think of himself more highly than he should think. Instead, think sensibly, as God has distributed a measure of faith to each one. [4] Now as we have many parts in one body, and all the parts do not have the same function,

[5] in the same way we who are many are one body in Christ and individually members of one another.

[6] According to the grace given to us, we have different gifts: If prophecy, use it according to the proportion of one's faith; [7] if service, use it in service; if teaching, in teaching; [8] if exhorting, in exhortation; giving, with generosity; leading, with diligence; showing mercy, with cheerfulness.

Cinnamon Chai Shortbread Cookies

YIELDS: 24 COOKIES

Cookies

1 cup unsalted butter, softened
¾ cup granulated sugar
½ teaspoon salt
½ teaspoon cinnamon
1 tablespoon chai tea, brewed
2¼ cups all-purpose flour

Glaze

2 tablespoons chai tea, brewed
1 cup confectioner's sugar

Directions

Using a mixer, cream together butter and sugar.

Add salt, cinnamon, and 1 tablespoon tea until combined.

Gradually add flour at a low speed. The mixture will be dry and crumbly at first, but will combine to form a soft dough.

Mold dough into a 10-inch log and cover tightly with plastic wrap. Refrigerate for at least one hour until firm.

Preheat oven to 350°F.

Once dough is firm, remove plastic wrap. With a serrated bread knife, cut log into half-inch slices. Line 2 cookie sheets with parchment paper and place slices 2 inches apart.

Bake 22 to 25 minutes, until the edges are golden brown.

While cookies cool, prepare glaze by mixing tea and sugar with a whisk, until smooth.

Spoon glaze over cooled cookies and allow glaze to set.

Serve with a warm mug of homemade chai.

06 GRACE DAY

Take this day to catch up on your reading,
pray, and rest in the presence of the Lord.

LORD, our Lord,
how magnificent is your name
throughout the earth!

PSALM 8:9

WEEK 1

WEEK 2

WEEK 3

07 WEEKLY TRUTH

Scripture is God-breathed and true.
When we memorize it, we carry the good
news of Jesus with us wherever we go.

Over the course of this study, we will memorize Ephesians
2:8–10. Let's begin by memorizing verse 8.

Write the passage out by hand, say it aloud, or test your
knowledge with a friend.

WEEK 1

WEEK 2

WEEK 3

For you are saved by grace through faith, and this is not from yourselves; it is God's gift—not from works, so that no one can boast. For we are his workmanship, created in Christ Jesus for good works, which God prepared ahead of time for us to do.

EPHESIANS 2:8–10

Response Questions

Ephesians 2:12–18

¹² At that time you were without Christ, excluded from the citizenship of Israel, and foreigners to the covenants of promise, without hope and without God in the world. ¹³ But now in Christ Jesus, you who were far away have been brought near by the blood of Christ. ¹⁴ For he is our peace, who made both groups one and tore down the dividing wall of hostility. In his flesh, ¹⁵ he made of no effect the law consisting of commands and expressed in regulations, so that he might create in himself one new man from the two, resulting in peace. ¹⁶ He did this so that he might reconcile both to God in one body through the cross by which he put the hostility to death. ¹⁷ He came and proclaimed the good news of peace to you who were far away and peace to those who were near. ¹⁸ For through him we both have access in one Spirit to the Father.

1. Reflect on the passage. What was your immediate reaction upon reading it? Did anything stand out to you?

2. What does unity in Christ look like in this passage?

notes

08 Paul's Ministry to the Gentiles

WEEK 1

WEEK 2

WEEK 3

Ephesians 3:1–13

PAUL'S MINISTRY TO THE GENTILES

¹ For this reason, I, Paul, the prisoner of Christ Jesus on behalf of you Gentiles— ² you have heard, haven't you, about the administration of God's grace that he gave to me for you? ³ The mystery was made known to me by revelation, as I have briefly written above. ⁴ By reading this you are able to understand my insight into the mystery of Christ. ⁵ This was not made known to people in other generations as it is now revealed to his holy apostles and prophets by the Spirit: ⁶ The Gentiles are coheirs, members of the same body, and partners in the promise in Christ Jesus through the gospel. ⁷ I was made a servant of this gospel by the gift of God's grace that was given to me by the working of his power.

⁸ This grace was given to me—the least of all the saints—to proclaim to the Gentiles the incalculable riches of Christ, ⁹ and to shed light for all about the administration of the mystery hidden for ages in God who created all things. ¹⁰ This is so that God's multi-faceted wisdom may now be made known through the church to the rulers and authorities in the heavens. ¹¹ This is according to his eternal purpose accomplished in Christ Jesus our Lord.

¹² In him we have boldness and confident access through faith in him.

¹³ So then I ask you not to be discouraged over my afflictions on your behalf, for they are your glory.

Romans 11

ISRAEL'S REJECTION NOT TOTAL

¹ I ask, then, has God rejected his people? Absolutely not! For I too am an Israelite, a descendant of Abraham, from the tribe of Benjamin. ² God has not rejected his people whom he foreknew. Or don't you know what the Scripture says in the passage about Elijah—how he pleads with God against Israel? ³ Lord, they have killed your prophets and torn down your altars. I am the only one left, and they are trying to take my life! ⁴ But what was God's answer to him? I have left seven thousand for myself who have not bowed down to Baal. ⁵ In the same way, then, there is also at the present time a remnant chosen by grace. ⁶ Now if by grace, then it is not by works; otherwise grace ceases to be grace.

⁷ What then? Israel did not find what it was looking for, but the elect did find it. The rest were hardened, ⁸ as it is written,

> God gave them a spirit of stupor,
> eyes that cannot see
> and ears that cannot hear,
> to this day.

⁹ And David says,

> Let their table become a snare and a trap,
> a pitfall and a retribution to them.
> ¹⁰ Let their eyes be darkened so that they cannot see,
> and their backs be bent continually.

ISRAEL'S REJECTION NOT FINAL

¹¹ I ask, then, have they stumbled so as to fall? Absolutely not! On the contrary, by their transgression, salvation has come to the Gentiles to make Israel jealous. ¹² Now if their transgression brings riches for the world, and their failure riches for the Gentiles, how much more will their fullness bring!

¹³ Now I am speaking to you Gentiles. Insofar as I am an apostle to the Gentiles, I magnify my ministry, ¹⁴ if I might somehow make my own people jealous and

save some of them. [15] For if their rejection brings reconciliation to the world, what will their acceptance mean but life from the dead? [16] Now if the firstfruits are holy, so is the whole batch. And if the root is holy, so are the branches.

[17] Now if some of the branches were broken off, and you, though a wild olive branch, were grafted in among them and have come to share in the rich root of the cultivated olive tree, [18] do not boast that you are better than those branches. But if you do boast—you do not sustain the root, but the root sustains you. [19] Then you will say, "Branches were broken off so that I might be grafted in." [20] True enough; they were broken off because of unbelief, but you stand by faith. Do not be arrogant, but beware, [21] because if God did not spare the natural branches, he will not spare you either. [22] Therefore, consider God's kindness and severity: severity toward those who have fallen but God's kindness toward you—if you remain in his kindness. Otherwise you too will be cut off. [23] And even they, if they do not remain in unbelief, will be grafted in, because God has the power to graft them in again. [24] For if you were cut off from your native wild olive tree and against nature were grafted into a cultivated olive tree, how much more will these—the natural branches—be grafted into their own olive tree?

[25] I don't want you to be ignorant of this mystery, brothers and sisters, so that you will not be conceited: A partial hardening has come upon Israel until the fullness of the Gentiles has come in. [26] And in this way all Israel will be saved, as it is written,

> The Deliverer will come from Zion;
> he will turn godlessness away from Jacob.
> [27] And this will be my covenant with them
> when I take away their sins.

[28] Regarding the gospel, they are enemies for your advantage, but regarding election, they are loved because of the patriarchs, [29] since God's gracious gifts and calling are irrevocable. [30] As you once disobeyed God but now have received mercy through their disobedience, [31] so they too have now disobeyed, resulting in mercy to you, so that they also may now receive mercy. [32] For God has imprisoned all in disobedience so that he may have mercy on all.

A HYMN OF PRAISE

> [33] Oh, the depth of the riches
> both of the wisdom and of the knowledge of God!
> How unsearchable his judgments
> and untraceable his ways!
> [34] For who has known the mind of the Lord?
> Or who has been his counselor?

³⁵ And who has ever given to God,
that he should be repaid?
³⁶ For from him and through him
and to him are all things.
To him be the glory forever. Amen.

Colossians 1:24–29

PAUL'S MINISTRY

²⁴ Now I rejoice in my sufferings for you, and I am completing in my flesh what is lacking in Christ's afflictions for his body, that is, the church. ²⁵ I have become its servant, according to God's commission that was given to me for you, to make the word of God fully known, ²⁶ the mystery hidden for ages and generations but now revealed to his saints.

²⁷ God wanted to make known among the Gentiles the glorious wealth of this mystery, which is Christ in you, the hope of glory.

²⁸ We proclaim him, warning and teaching everyone with all wisdom, so that we may present everyone mature in Christ. ²⁹ I labor for this, striving with his strength that works powerfully in me.

notes

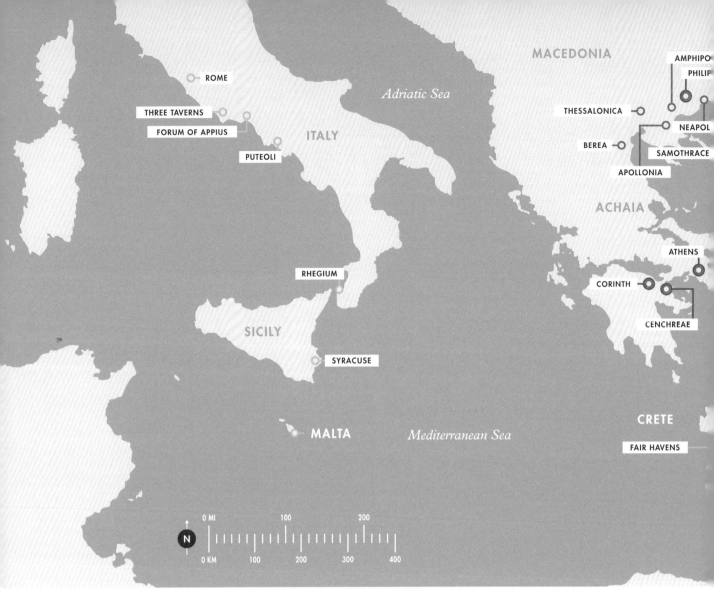

Paul's Missionary Journeys

In the book of Acts, Jesus tells His disciples to share the gospel with people "in Jerusalem, in all Judea and Samaria, and to the end of the earth" (1:8). Paul and his friends were the first who took on the challenge of traveling to places like Ephesus, sharing the gospel and encouraging churches as their numbers grew (Ac 18:19–21). He later spent two years in Ephesus on his third missionary journey, debating with the people there about the kingdom of God (Ac 19). On this map, you can see the places Paul visited on each of his missionary journeys.

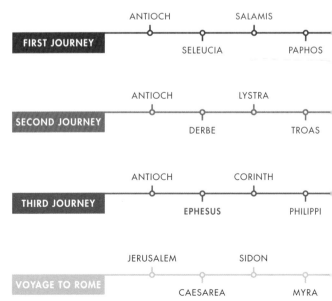

FIRST JOURNEY

ANTIOCH · SALAMIS
SELEUCIA · PAPHOS

SECOND JOURNEY

ANTIOCH · LYSTRA
DERBE · TROAS

THIRD JOURNEY

ANTIOCH · CORINTH
EPHESUS · PHILIPPI

VOYAGE TO ROME

JERUSALEM · SIDON
CAESAREA · MYRA

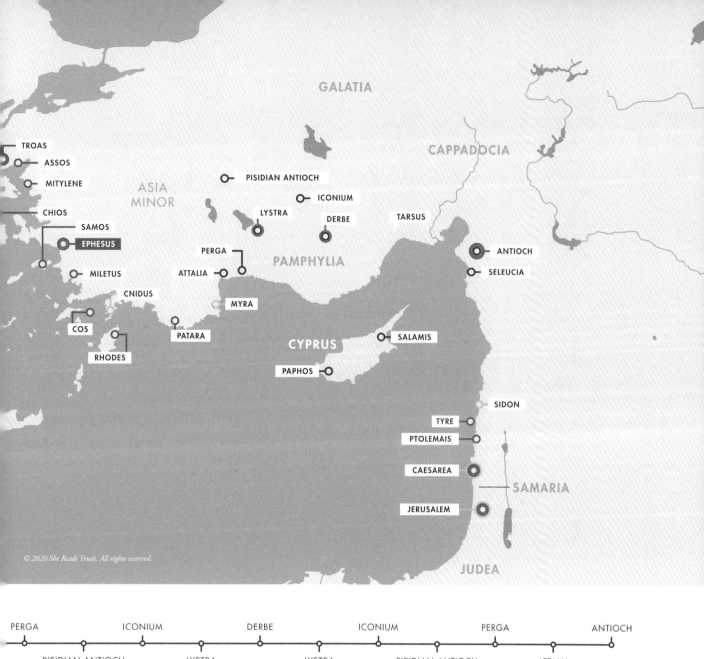

GALATIA

CAPPADOCIA

TROAS
ASSOS
MITYLENE

ASIA
MINOR

PISIDIAN ANTIOCH

ICONIUM

CHIOS

LYSTRA

DERBE

TARSUS

SAMOS
EPHESUS

PERGA

MILETUS
CNIDUS

ATTALIA

PAMPHYLIA

ANTIOCH
SELEUCIA

MYRA

COS

PATARA

CYPRUS

SALAMIS

RHODES

PAPHOS

SIDON
TYRE
PTOLEMAIS

CAESAREA
SAMARIA

JERUSALEM

JUDEA

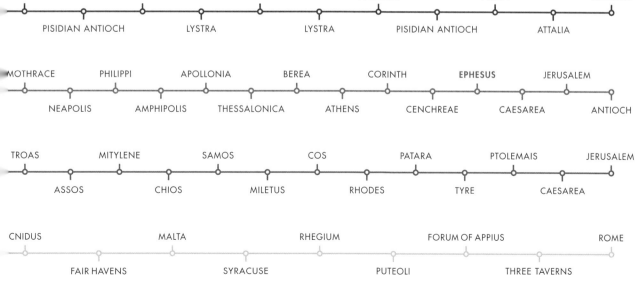

PERGA		ICONIUM		DERBE		ICONIUM		PERGA		ANTIOCH
	PISIDIAN ANTIOCH		LYSTRA		LYSTRA		PISIDIAN ANTIOCH		ATTALIA	

SAMOTHRACE		PHILIPPI		APOLLONIA		BEREA		CORINTH		EPHESUS		JERUSALEM
	NEAPOLIS		AMPHIPOLIS		THESSALONICA		ATHENS		CENCHREAE		CAESAREA		ANTIOCH

TROAS		MITYLENE		SAMOS		COS		PATARA		PTOLEMAIS		JERUSALEM
	ASSOS		CHIOS		MILETUS		RHODES		TYRE		CAESAREA	

CNIDUS		MALTA		RHEGIUM		FORUM OF APPIUS		ROME
	FAIR HAVENS		SYRACUSE		PUTEOLI		THREE TAVERNS	

55

09 Prayer for Spiritual Power

WEEK 1

WEEK 2

WEEK 3

Ephesians 3:14–21

PRAYER FOR SPIRITUAL POWER

14 For this reason I kneel before the Father 15 from whom every family in heaven and on earth is named. 16 I pray that he may grant you, according to the riches of his glory, to be strengthened with power in your inner being through his Spirit, 17 and that Christ may dwell in your hearts through faith. I pray that you, being rooted and firmly established in love, 18 may be able to comprehend with all the saints what is the length and width, height and depth of God's love, 19 and to know Christ's love that surpasses knowledge, so that you may be filled with all the fullness of God.

20 Now to him who is able to do above and beyond all that we ask or think according to the power that works in us— 21 to him be glory in the church and in Christ Jesus to all generations, forever and ever. Amen.

Psalm 103

THE FORGIVING GOD

Of David.

¹ My soul, bless the LORD,
and all that is within me, bless his holy name.
² My soul, bless the LORD,
and do not forget all his benefits.

³ He forgives all your iniquity;
he heals all your diseases.
⁴ He redeems your life from the Pit;
he crowns you with faithful love and compassion.
⁵ He satisfies you with good things;
your youth is renewed like the eagle.

⁶ The LORD executes acts of righteousness
and justice for all the oppressed.
⁷ He revealed his ways to Moses,
his deeds to the people of Israel.
⁸ The LORD is compassionate and gracious,
slow to anger and abounding in faithful love.
⁹ He will not always accuse us
or be angry forever.
¹⁰ He has not dealt with us as our sins deserve
or repaid us according to our iniquities.

¹¹ For as high as the heavens are above the earth,
so great is his faithful love
toward those who fear him.
¹² As far as the east is from the west,
so far has he removed
our transgressions from us.
¹³ As a father has compassion on his children,
so the LORD has compassion on those who fear him.
¹⁴ For he knows what we are made of,
remembering that we are dust.

¹⁵ As for man, his days are like grass—
he blooms like a flower of the field;
¹⁶ when the wind passes over it, it vanishes,
and its place is no longer known.
¹⁷ But from eternity to eternity
the LORD's faithful love is toward those who fear him,
and his righteousness toward the grandchildren
¹⁸ of those who keep his covenant,
who remember to observe his precepts.
¹⁹ The LORD has established his throne in heaven,
and his kingdom rules over all.

²⁰ Bless the LORD,
all his angels of great strength,
who do his word,
obedient to his command.
²¹ Bless the LORD, all his armies,
his servants who do his will.
²² Bless the LORD, all his works
in all the places where he rules.
My soul, bless the LORD!

Philippians 4:12–13

¹² I know both how to make do with little, and I know how to make do with a lot. In any and all circumstances I have learned the secret of being content—whether well fed or hungry, whether in abundance or in need.

¹³ I am able to do all things through him who strengthens me.

noTes

10 Unity and Diversity in the Body of Christ

WEEK 1

WEEK 2

WEEK 3

Ephesians 4:1–16

UNITY AND DIVERSITY IN THE BODY OF CHRIST

[1] Therefore I, the prisoner in the Lord, urge you to live worthy of the calling you have received, [2] with all humility and gentleness, with patience, bearing with one another in love, [3] making every effort to keep the unity of the Spirit through the bond of peace. [4] There is one body and one Spirit—just as you were called to one hope at your calling— [5] one Lord, one faith, one baptism, [6] one God and Father of all, who is above all and through all and in all.

[7] Now grace was given to each one of us according to the measure of Christ's gift. [8] For it says:

> When he ascended on high,
> he took the captives captive;
> he gave gifts to people.

[9] But what does "he ascended" mean except that he also descended to the lower parts of the earth? [10] The one who descended is also the one who ascended far above all the heavens, to fill all things. [11] And he himself gave some to be apostles, some prophets, some evangelists, some pastors and teachers, [12] equipping the saints for the work of ministry, to build up the body of Christ, [13] until we all reach unity in the faith and in the knowledge of God's Son, growing into maturity with a stature measured by Christ's fullness.[14] Then we will no longer be little children, tossed by the waves and blown around by every wind of teaching, by human cunning with cleverness in the techniques of deceit. [15] But speaking the truth in love, let us grow in every way into him who is the head—Christ. [16] From him the whole body, fitted and knit together by every supporting ligament, promotes the growth of the body for building up itself in love by the proper working of each individual part.

Acts 2:42–47

A GENEROUS AND GROWING CHURCH

[42] They devoted themselves to the apostles' teaching, to the fellowship, to the breaking of bread, and to prayer.

[43] Everyone was filled with awe, and many wonders and signs were being performed through the apostles. [44] Now all the believers were together and held all things in common. [45] They sold their possessions and property and distributed the proceeds to all, as any had need. [46] Every day they devoted themselves to meeting together in the temple, and broke bread from house to house. They ate their food with joyful and sincere hearts, [47] praising God and enjoying the favor of all the people. Every day the Lord added to their number those who were being saved.

1 Corinthians 12:12–27

UNITY YET DIVERSITY IN THE BODY

[12] For just as the body is one and has many parts, and all the parts of that body, though many, are one body—so also is Christ. [13] For we were all baptized by one Spirit into one body—whether Jews or Greeks, whether slaves or free—and we were all given one Spirit to drink. [14] Indeed, the body is not one part but many. [15] If the foot should say, "Because I'm not a hand, I don't belong to the body," it

is not for that reason any less a part of the body. [16] And if the ear should say, "Because I'm not an eye, I don't belong to the body," it is not for that reason any less a part of the body. [17] If the whole body were an eye, where would the hearing be? If the whole body were an ear, where would the sense of smell be? [18] But as it is, God has arranged each one of the parts in the body just as he wanted. [19] And if they were all the same part, where would the body be? [20] As it is, there are many parts, but one body. [21] The eye cannot say to the hand, "I don't need you!" Or again, the head can't say to the feet, "I don't need you!" [22] On the contrary, those parts of the body that are weaker are indispensable. [23] And those parts of the body that we consider less honorable, we clothe these with greater honor, and our unrespectable parts are treated with greater respect, [24] which our respectable parts do not need.

Instead, God has put the body together, giving greater honor to the less honorable, [25] so that there would be no division in the body, but that the members would have the same concern for each other. [26] So if one member suffers, all the members suffer with it; if one member is honored, all the members rejoice with it.

[27] Now you are the body of Christ, and individual members of it.

notes

Spiritual Gifts

Spiritual gifts are one way God equips the Church for the life and work He calls us to. These gifts range from essentials for the Christian life, to miraculous abilities, to roles and skills necessary for the ongoing ministry of the Church. While the gifts on this list vary in type, they all share one distinctive quality: they come from the Holy Spirit.

1

ESSENTIAL GIFTS

Qualities given to all believers everywhere that are necessary for living the Christian life

2

DYNAMIC GIFTS

Special abilities given by the Holy Spirit for the specific purpose of delivering or validating a message from God

3

FUNCTIONAL GIFTS

Roles and abilities needed for the ongoing structure and ministry of the Church on earth

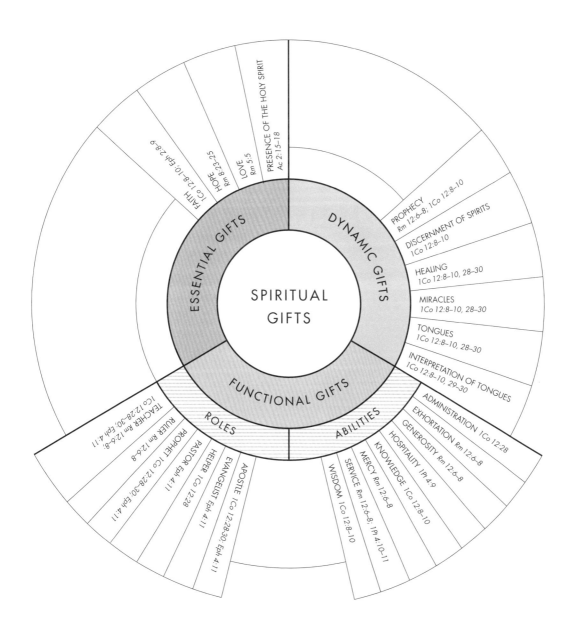

SPIRITUAL GIFTS

ESSENTIAL GIFTS
- PRESENCE OF THE HOLY SPIRIT Ac 2:15–18
- LOVE Rm 5:5
- HOPE Rm 8:23–25
- FAITH 1Co 12:8–10; Eph 2:8–9

DYNAMIC GIFTS
- PROPHECY Rm 12:6–8; 1Co 12:8–10
- DISCERNMENT OF SPIRITS 1Co 12:8–10
- HEALING 1Co 12:8–10, 28–30
- MIRACLES 1Co 12:8–10, 28–30
- TONGUES 1Co 12:8–10, 28–30
- INTERPRETATION OF TONGUES 1Co 12:8–10, 29–30

FUNCTIONAL GIFTS

ROLES
- TEACHER Rm 12:6–8; 1Co 12:28–30; Eph 4:11
- RULER Rm 12:6–8
- PROPHET 1Co 12:6–8
- PASTOR Eph 4:11
- HELPER 1Co 12:28
- EVANGELIST Eph 4:11
- APOSTLE 1Co 12:28–30; Eph 4:11

ABILITIES
- ADMINISTRATION 1Co 12:28
- EXHORTATION Rm 12:6–8
- GENEROSITY Rm 12:6–8
- HOSPITALITY 1Pt 4:9
- KNOWLEDGE 1Co 12:8–10
- MERCY Rm 12:6–8
- SERVICE Rm 12:6–8; 1Pt 4:10–11
- WISDOM 1Co 12:8–10

Some Christian traditions believe that the miraculous and revelatory gifts ceased with the end of the apostolic age. Others hold they still are accessible today.

11 Living the New Life

Ephesians 4:17–32

LIVING THE NEW LIFE

[17] Therefore, I say this and testify in the Lord: You should no longer live as the Gentiles live, in the futility of their thoughts. [18] They are darkened in their understanding, excluded from the life of God, because of the ignorance that is in them and because of the hardness of their hearts. [19] They became callous and gave themselves over to promiscuity for the practice of every kind of impurity with a desire for more and more.

[20] But that is not how you came to know Christ, [21] assuming you heard about him and were taught by him, as the truth is in Jesus, [22] to take off your former way of life, the old self that is corrupted by deceitful desires, [23] to be renewed in the spirit of your minds, [24] and to put on the new self, the one created according to God's likeness in righteousness and purity of the truth.

[25] Therefore, putting away lying, speak the truth, each one to his neighbor, because we are members of one another. [26] Be angry and do not sin. Don't let the sun go down on your anger, [27] and don't give the devil an opportunity.

28 Let the thief no longer steal. Instead, he is to do honest work with his own hands, so that he has something to share with anyone in need. 29 No foul language should come from your mouth, but only what is good for building up someone in need, so that it gives grace to those who hear. 30 And don't grieve God's Holy Spirit. You were sealed by him for the day of redemption. 31 Let all bitterness, anger and wrath, shouting and slander be removed from you, along with all malice. 32 And be kind and compassionate to one another, forgiving one another, just as God also forgave you in Christ.

Ephesians 5:1–5

1 Therefore, be imitators of God, as dearly loved children, 2 and walk in love, as Christ also loved us and gave himself for us, a sacrificial and fragrant offering to God. 3 But sexual immorality and any impurity or greed should not even be heard of among you, as is proper for saints. 4 Obscene and foolish talking or crude joking are not suitable, but rather giving thanks. 5 For know and recognize this: Every sexually immoral or impure or greedy person, who is an idolater, does not have an inheritance in the kingdom of Christ and of God.

Hosea 1:10

Yet the number of the Israelites
will be like the sand of the sea,
which cannot be measured or counted.
And in the place where they were told:
You are not my people,
they will be called: Sons of the living God.

James 3
CONTROLLING THE TONGUE

1 Not many should become teachers, my brothers, because you know that we will receive a stricter judgment. 2 For we all stumble in many ways. If anyone does not stumble in what he says, he is mature, able also to control the whole body. 3 Now if we put bits into the mouths of horses so that they obey us, we direct their whole bodies. 4 And consider ships: Though very large and driven by fierce winds, they are guided by a very small rudder wherever the will of the pilot directs. 5 So too, though the tongue is a small part of the body, it boasts great things. Consider how a small fire sets ablaze a large forest. 6 And the tongue is a fire. The tongue, a world of unrighteousness, is placed among our members. It stains the whole body, sets the course of life on fire, and is itself set on fire by hell. 7 Every kind of animal, bird, reptile, and fish is tamed and has been tamed by humankind, 8 but no one can tame the tongue. It is a restless evil, full of deadly poison. 9 With the tongue we bless our Lord and Father, and with it we curse people who are made in God's likeness. 10 Blessing and cursing come out of the same mouth. My brothers and sisters, these things should not be this way. 11 Does a spring pour out sweet and bitter water from the same opening? 12 Can a fig tree produce olives, my brothers and sisters, or a grapevine produce figs? Neither can a saltwater spring yield fresh water.

THE WISDOM FROM ABOVE

13 Who among you is wise and understanding? By his good conduct he should show that his works are done in the gentleness that comes from wisdom. 14 But if you have bitter envy and selfish ambition in your heart, don't boast and deny the truth. 15 Such wisdom does not come down from above but is earthly, unspiritual, demonic. 16 For where there is envy and selfish ambition, there is disorder and every evil practice. 17 But the wisdom from above is first pure, then peace-loving, gentle, compliant, full of mercy and good fruits, unwavering, without pretense. 18 And the fruit of righteousness is sown in peace by those who cultivate peace.

notes

Live as children of light…

12 Light Versus Darkness

○ WEEK 1

● WEEK 2

○ WEEK 3

Ephesians 5:6–14

LIGHT VERSUS DARKNESS

[6] Let no one deceive you with empty arguments, for God's wrath is coming on the disobedient because of these things. [7] Therefore, do not become their partners. [8] For you were once darkness, but now you are light in the Lord. Live as children of light— [9] for the fruit of the light consists of all goodness, righteousness, and truth— [10] testing what is pleasing to the Lord. [11] Don't participate in the fruitless works of darkness, but instead expose them. [12] For it is shameful even to mention what is done by them in secret. [13] Everything exposed by the light is made visible, [14] for what makes everything visible is light. Therefore it is said:

Get up, sleeper, and rise up from the dead,
and Christ will shine on you.

Psalm 36:9

For the wellspring of life is with you.
By means of your light we see light.

1 John 1:5–10

FELLOWSHIP WITH GOD

[5] This is the message we have heard from him and declare to you: God is light, and there is absolutely no darkness in him. [6] If we say, "We have fellowship with him," and yet we walk in darkness, we are lying and are not practicing the truth.

[7] If we walk in the light as he himself is in the light, we have fellowship with one another,

and the blood of Jesus his Son cleanses us from all sin. [8] If we say, "We have no sin," we are deceiving ourselves, and the truth is not in us. [9] If we confess our sins, he is faithful and righteous to forgive us our sins and to cleanse us from all unrighteousness. [10] If we say, "We have not sinned," we make him a liar, and his word is not in us.

notes

13 GRACE DAY

Take this day to catch up on your reading,
pray, and rest in the presence of the Lord.

Now these three remain: faith, hope, and love—but the greatest of these is love.

1 CORINTHIANS 13:13

14 WEEKLY TRUTH

Scripture is God-breathed and true.
When we memorize it, we carry the good
news of Jesus with us wherever we go.

Over the course of this study, we are memorizing Ephesians
2:8–10. Last week, we memorized verse 8, the first part of
the key verse for Ephesians. This week, we'll add verse 9.

Write the passage out by hand, say it aloud, or test your
knowledge with a friend.

○ WEEK 1

● WEEK 2

○ WEEK 3

For you are saved by grace through faith, and this is not from yourselves; it is God's gift—not from works, so that no one can boast. For we are his workmanship, created in Christ Jesus for good works, which God prepared ahead of time for us to do.

EPHESIANS 2:8–10

Response Questions

Ephesians 4:1–6

¹ Therefore I, the prisoner in the Lord, urge you to live worthy of the calling you have received, ² with all humility and gentleness, with patience, bearing with one another in love, ³ making every effort to keep the unity of the Spirit through the bond of peace. ⁴ There is one body and one Spirit—just as you were called to one hope at your calling— ⁵ one Lord, one faith, one baptism, ⁶ one God and Father of all, who is above all and through all and in all.

1. Reflect on the passage. What was your immediate reaction upon reading it? Did anything stand out to you?

2. What does unity in Christ look like in this passage?

notes

15 Consistency in the Christian Life

○ WEEK 1

○ WEEK 2

● WEEK 3

Ephesians 5:15–21

CONSISTENCY IN THE CHRISTIAN LIFE

[15] Pay careful attention, then, to how you live—not as unwise people but as wise— [16] making the most of the time, because the days are evil. [17] So don't be foolish, but understand what the Lord's will is. [18] And don't get drunk with wine, which leads to reckless living, but be filled by the Spirit: [19] speaking to one another in psalms, hymns, and spiritual songs, singing and making music with your heart to the Lord, [20] giving thanks always for everything to God the Father in the name of our Lord Jesus Christ, [21] submitting to one another in the fear of Christ.

Amos 5:4–15

SEEK GOD AND LIVE

[4] For the LORD says to the house of Israel:

Seek me and live!
[5] Do not seek Bethel
or go to Gilgal
or journey to Beer-sheba,
for Gilgal will certainly go into exile,

and Bethel will come to nothing.
⁶ Seek the LORD and live,
or he will spread like fire
throughout the house of Joseph;
it will consume everything
with no one at Bethel to extinguish it.
⁷ Those who turn justice into wormwood
also throw righteousness to the ground.

⁸ The one who made the Pleiades and Orion,
who turns darkness into dawn
and darkens day into night,
who summons the water of the sea
and pours it out over the surface of the earth—
the LORD is his name.
⁹ He brings destruction on the strong,
and it falls on the fortress.

¹⁰ They hate the one who convicts the guilty
at the city gate,
and they despise the one who speaks with integrity.
¹¹ Therefore, because you trample on the poor
and exact a grain tax from him,
you will never live in the houses of cut stone
you have built;
you will never drink the wine
from the lush vineyards
you have planted.
¹² For I know your crimes are many
and your sins innumerable.
They oppress the righteous, take a bribe,
and deprive the poor of justice at the city gates.
¹³ Therefore, those who have insight will keep silent
at such a time,
for the days are evil.

¹⁴ Pursue good and not evil
so that you may live,
and the LORD, the God of Armies,
will be with you
as you have claimed.
¹⁵ Hate evil and love good;
establish justice in the city gate.
Perhaps the LORD, the God of Armies, will be gracious
to the remnant of Joseph.

Colossians 3:12–17

THE CHRISTIAN LIFE

¹² Therefore, as God's chosen ones, holy and dearly loved, put on compassion, kindness, humility, gentleness, and patience, ¹³ bearing with one another and forgiving one another if anyone has a grievance against another. Just as the Lord has forgiven you, so you are also to forgive. ¹⁴ Above all, put on love, which is the perfect bond of unity. ¹⁵ And let the peace of Christ, to which you were also called in one body, rule your hearts. And be thankful. ¹⁶ Let the word of Christ dwell richly among you, in all wisdom teaching and admonishing one another through psalms, hymns, and spiritual songs, singing to God with gratitude in your hearts.

¹⁷ And whatever you do, in word or in deed, do everything in the name of the Lord Jesus,

giving thanks to God the Father through him.

notes

Each one of you is to love his wife as himself,
and the wife is to respect her husband.

EPHESIANS 5:33

16 Wives and Husbands

WEEK 1

WEEK 2

WEEK 3

Ephesians 5:22–33

WIVES AND HUSBANDS

[22] Wives, submit to your husbands as to the Lord, [23] because the husband is the head of the wife as Christ is the head of the church. He is the Savior of the body. [24] Now as the church submits to Christ, so also wives are to submit to their husbands in everything. [25] Husbands, love your wives, just as Christ loved the church and gave himself for her [26] to make her holy, cleansing her with the washing of water by the word. [27] He did this to present the church to himself in splendor, without spot or wrinkle or anything like that, but holy and blameless. [28] In the same way, husbands are to love their wives as their own bodies. He who loves his wife loves himself. [29] For no one ever hates his own flesh but provides and cares for it, just as Christ does for the church, [30] since we are members of his body. [31] For this reason a man will leave his father and mother and be joined to his wife, and the two will become one flesh. [32] This mystery is profound, but I am talking about Christ and the church. [33] To sum up, each one of you is to love his wife as himself, and the wife is to respect her husband.

Genesis 2:4–25

[4] These are the records of the heavens and the earth, concerning their creation. At the time that the LORD God made the earth and the heavens, [5] no shrub of the field had yet grown on the land, and no plant of the field had yet sprouted, for the LORD God had not made it rain on the land, and there was no man to work the ground. [6] But mist would come up from the earth and water all the ground. [7] Then the LORD God formed the man out of the dust from the ground and breathed the breath of life into his nostrils, and the man became a living being.

[8] The LORD God planted a garden in Eden, in the east, and there he placed the man he had formed. [9] The LORD God caused to grow out of the ground every tree pleasing in appearance and good for food, including the tree of life in the middle of the garden, as well as the tree of the knowledge of good and evil.

[10] A river went out from Eden to water the garden. From there it divided and became the source of four rivers. [11] The name of the first is Pishon, which flows through the entire land of Havilah, where there is gold. [12] Gold from that land is pure; bdellium and onyx are also there. [13] The name of the second river is Gihon, which flows through the entire land of Cush. [14] The name of the third river is Tigris, which runs east of Assyria. And the fourth river is the Euphrates.

[15] The LORD God took the man and placed him in the garden of Eden to work it and watch over it. [16] And the LORD God commanded the man, "You are free to eat from any tree of the garden, [17] but you must not eat from the tree of the knowledge of good and evil, for on the day you eat from it, you will certainly die." [18] Then the LORD God said, "It is not good for the man to be alone. I will make a helper corresponding to him." [19] The LORD God formed out of the ground every wild animal and every bird of the sky, and brought each to the man to see what he would call it. And whatever the man called a living creature, that was its name. [20] The man gave names to all the livestock, to the birds of the sky, and to every wild animal; but for the man no helper was found corresponding to him. [21] So the LORD God

caused a deep sleep to come over the man, and he slept. God took one of his ribs and closed the flesh at that place. [22] Then the LORD God made the rib he had taken from the man into a woman and brought her to the man. [23] And the man said:

> This one, at last, is bone of my bone
> and flesh of my flesh;
> this one will be called "woman,"
> for she was taken from man.

[24] This is why a man leaves his father and mother and bonds with his wife, and they become one flesh. [25] Both the man and his wife were naked, yet felt no shame.

Colossians 3:18–25

[18] Wives, submit yourselves to your husbands, as is fitting in the Lord. [19] Husbands, love your wives and don't be bitter toward them. [20] Children, obey your parents in everything, for this pleases the Lord. [21] Fathers, do not exasperate your children, so that they won't become discouraged. [22] Slaves, obey your human masters in everything. Don't work only while being watched, as people-pleasers, but work wholeheartedly, fearing the Lord.

[23] Whatever you do, do it from the heart, as something done for the Lord and not for people,

[24] knowing that you will receive the reward of an inheritance from the Lord. You serve the Lord Christ. [25] For the wrongdoer will be paid back for whatever wrong he has done, and there is no favoritism.

notes

17 Children and Parents

WEEK 1

WEEK 2

WEEK 3

Ephesians 6:1–4

CHILDREN AND PARENTS

¹ Children, obey your parents in the Lord, because this is right. ² Honor your father and mother, which is the first commandment with a promise, ³ so that it may go well with you and that you may have a long life in the land. ⁴ Fathers, don't stir up anger in your children, but bring them up in the training and instruction of the Lord.

Exodus 20:12

Honor your father and your mother so that you may have a long life in the land that the LORD your God is giving you.

Matthew 15:1–9

THE TRADITION OF THE ELDERS

¹ Then Jesus was approached by Pharisees and scribes from Jerusalem, who asked, ² "Why do your disciples break the tradition of the elders? For they don't wash their hands when they eat."

³ He answered them, "Why do you break God's commandment because of your tradition? ⁴ For God said: Honor your father and your mother; and, Whoever speaks evil of father or mother must be put to death. ⁵ But you say, 'Whoever tells his father or mother, "Whatever benefit you might have received from me is a gift committed to the temple," ⁶ he does not have to honor his father.' In this way, you have nullified the word of God because of your tradition. ⁷ Hypocrites! Isaiah prophesied correctly about you when he said:

⁸ This people honors me with their lips,
but their heart is far from me.
⁹ They worship me in vain,
teaching as doctrines human commands."

18 Slaves and Masters

Ephesians 6:5–9

SLAVES AND MASTERS

⁵ Slaves, obey your human masters with fear and trembling, in the sincerity of your heart, as you would Christ. ⁶ Don't work only while being watched, as people-pleasers, but as slaves of Christ, do God's will from your heart. ⁷ Serve with a good attitude, as to the Lord and not to people, ⁸ knowing that whatever good each one does, slave or free, he will receive this back from the Lord. ⁹ And masters, treat your slaves the same way, without threatening them, because you know that both their Master and yours is in heaven, and there is no favoritism with him.

Galatians 3:27–29

SONS AND HEIRS

²⁷ For those of you who were baptized into Christ have been clothed with Christ. ²⁸ There is no Jew or Greek, slave or free, male and female; since you are all one in Christ Jesus. ²⁹ And if you belong to Christ, then you are Abraham's seed, heirs according to the promise.

Philemon 8–22

[8] For this reason, although I have great boldness in Christ to command you to do what is right, [9] I appeal to you, instead, on the basis of love. I, Paul, as an elderly man and now also as a prisoner of Christ Jesus, [10] appeal to you for my son, Onesimus. I became his father while I was in chains. [11] Once he was useless to you, but now he is useful both to you and to me. [12] I am sending him back to you—I am sending my very own heart. [13] I wanted to keep him with me, so that in my imprisonment for the gospel he might serve me in your place. [14] But I didn't want to do anything without your consent, so that your good deed might not be out of obligation, but of your own free will. [15] For perhaps this is why he was separated from you for a brief time, so that you might get him back permanently,

[16] no longer as a slave, but more than a slave—as a dearly loved brother.

He is especially so to me, but how much more to you, both in the flesh and in the Lord.

[17] So if you consider me a partner, welcome him as you would me. [18] And if he has wronged you in any way, or owes you anything, charge that to my account. [19] I, Paul, write this with my own hand: I will repay it—not to mention to you that you owe me even your very self. [20] Yes, brother, may I benefit from you in the Lord; refresh my heart in Christ. [21] Since I am confident of your obedience, I am writing to you, knowing that you will do even more than I say. [22] Meanwhile, also prepare a guest room for me, since I hope that through your prayers I will be restored to you.

notes

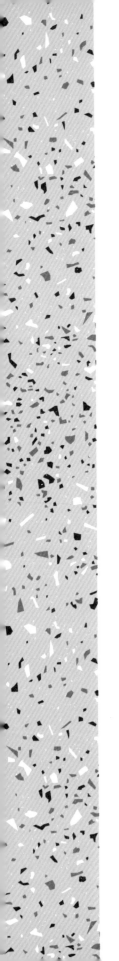

Spiritual Warfare

The Bible tells us there is more to the universe than what we can see with our eyes and touch with our hands. In Ephesians, we read that there is an unseen spiritual realm where a war is being waged (Eph 6:12). Though it is beyond our senses most of the time, we are all engaged in the battle against evil nonetheless. In order for us to better understand this ongoing spiritual battle, we go to Scripture.

SCRIPTURE TELLS US:

Our battle is…

not against other people.
EPH 6:12

a good fight of faith.
1TM 6:12

ongoing, though the decisive battle was won on the cross.
COL 2:15

to serve as Christ's ambassadors, helping in His ministry to reconcile people from every tribe, tongue, and nation to Him.
2CO 5:16–21; RV 7:9–12

an offensive operation, rather than a defensive one; the gates of hell will not prevail.
MT 16:17–19

Our enemies include…

the devil, who schemes against us, looking to devour whom he may.
2 CO 2:11; 1PT 5:8

our flesh, which opposes the Holy Spirit at work within us to imprison us in our sin.
RM 7:23; GL 5:17

the world, which is no friend of God and hates those who follow Jesus.
JN 15:19–20; JMS 4:4

territorial spiritual forces, who influence world events and are variously described as rulers, authorities, principalities, and powers.
1CO 2:6–8; EPH 3:10; 6:12; DN 10:13

Our full spiritual armor includes...

the "belt of truth."
EPH 6:14 ESV

the "breastplate of righteousness."
EPH 6:14 ESV; IS 59:17

sandals ready with "the gospel of peace."
EPH 6:15

the "shield of faith."
EPH 6:16

the "helmet of salvation."
EPH 6:17; 1TH 5:8; IS 59:17

the "sword of the Spirit—which is the word of God."
EPH 6:17–18; HEB 4:12

Our strategy is to...

put on our spiritual armor and take our stand.
EPH 6:13

defend against the devil, and he will withdraw.
JMS 4:7

love God, rather than the things of the world.
1JN 2:15; JN 15:18–25

sanctify ourselves with truth, which is the word of God.
JN 17:17

put to death our earthly desires and walk by the Spirit.
GL 5:24–25; COL 3:5

renew our minds in order to discern God's will.
RM 12:2

overcome evil with good.
RM 12:21

19 Christian Warfare

Ephesians 6:10–24

CHRISTIAN WARFARE

¹⁰ Finally, be strengthened by the Lord and by his vast strength. ¹¹ Put on the full armor of God so that you can stand against the schemes of the devil. ¹² For our struggle is not against flesh and blood, but against the rulers, against the authorities, against the cosmic powers of this darkness, against evil, spiritual forces in the heavens. ¹³ For this reason take up the full armor of God, so that you may be able to resist in the evil day, and having prepared everything, to take your stand. ¹⁴ Stand, therefore, with truth like a belt around your waist, righteousness like armor on your chest, ¹⁵ and your feet sandaled with readiness for the gospel of peace. ¹⁶ In every situation take up the shield of faith with which you can extinguish all the flaming arrows of the evil one. ¹⁷ Take the helmet of salvation and the sword of the Spirit—which is the word of God. ¹⁸ Pray

at all times in the Spirit with every prayer and request, and stay alert with all perseverance and intercession for all the saints. [19] Pray also for me, that the message may be given to me when I open my mouth to make known with boldness the mystery of the gospel. [20] For this I am an ambassador in chains. Pray that I might be bold enough to speak about it as I should.

PAUL'S FAREWELL

[21] Tychicus, our dearly loved brother and faithful servant in the Lord, will tell you all the news about me so that you may be informed. [22] I am sending him to you for this very reason, to let you know how we are and to encourage your hearts.

[23] Peace to the brothers and sisters, and love with faith, from God the Father and the Lord Jesus Christ. [24] Grace be with all who have undying love for our Lord Jesus Christ.

Isaiah 59:12–17

[12] For our transgressions have multiplied before you,
and our sins testify against us.
For our transgressions are with us,
and we know our iniquities:
[13] transgression and deception against the LORD,
turning away from following our God,
speaking oppression and revolt,
conceiving and uttering lying words from the heart.
[14] Justice is turned back,
and righteousness stands far off.
For truth has stumbled in the public square,
and honesty cannot enter.
[15] Truth is missing,
and whoever turns from evil is plundered.
The LORD saw that there was no justice,
and he was offended.
[16] He saw that there was no man—
he was amazed that there was no one interceding;
so his own arm brought salvation,
and his own righteousness supported him.

[17] He put on righteousness as body armor,
and a helmet of salvation on his head;
he put on garments of vengeance for clothing,
and he wrapped himself in zeal as in a cloak.

1 Thessalonians 5:5–11

[5] For you are all children of light and children of the day. We do not belong to the night or the darkness. [6] So then, let us not sleep, like the rest, but let us stay awake and be self-controlled. [7] For those who sleep, sleep at night, and those who get drunk, get drunk at night. [8] But since we belong to the day, let us be self-controlled and put on the armor of faith and love, and a helmet of the hope of salvation. [9] For God did not appoint us to wrath, but to obtain salvation through our Lord Jesus Christ, [10] who died for us, so that whether we are awake or asleep, we may live together with him. [11] Therefore encourage one another and build each other up as you are already doing.

notes

20 GRACE DAY

Take this day to catch up on your reading,
pray, and rest in the presence of the Lord.

Whatever you do, do it from the
heart, as something done for the
Lord and not for people.

COLOSSIANS 3:23

WEEK 1

WEEK 2

WEEK 3

21 WEEKLY TRUTH

Scripture is God-breathed and true.
When we memorize it, we carry the good
news of Jesus with us wherever we go.

Over the course of this study, we have worked on memorizing
Ephesians 2:8–10. This week, we'll wrap up by memorizing
verse 10.

Write the full passage out by hand, say it aloud, or test your
knowledge with a friend.

WEEK 1

WEEK 2

WEEK 3

For you are saved by grace through faith, and this is not from yourselves; it is God's gift—not from works, so that no one can boast. For we are his workmanship, created in Christ Jesus for good works, which God prepared ahead of time for us to do.

EPHESIANS 2:8–10

Response Questions

Ephesians 5:15–21

¹⁵ Pay careful attention, then, to how you live—not as unwise people but as wise— ¹⁶ making the most of the time, because the days are evil. ¹⁷ So don't be foolish, but understand what the Lord's will is. ¹⁸ And don't get drunk with wine, which leads to reckless living, but be filled by the Spirit: ¹⁹ speaking to one another in psalms, hymns, and spiritual songs, singing and making music with your heart to the Lord, ²⁰ giving thanks always for everything to God the Father in the name of our Lord Jesus Christ, ²¹ submitting to one another in the fear of Christ.

1 Reflect on the passage. What was your immediate reaction upon reading it? Did anything stand out to you?

2 What does unity in Christ look like in this passage?

notes

CSB BOOK ABBREVIATIONS

OLD TESTAMENT

Genesis – Gn
Exodus – Ex
Leviticus – Lv
Numbers – Nm
Deuteronomy – Dt
Joshua – Jos
Judges – Jdg
Ruth – Ru
1 Samuel – 1Sm
2 Samuel – 2Sm
1 Kings – 1Kg
2 Kings – 2Kg
1 Chronicles – 1Ch
2 Chronicles – 2Ch
Ezra – Ezr
Nehemiah – Neh
Esther – Est
Job – Jb
Psalms – Ps
Proverbs – Pr
Ecclesiastes – Ec
Song of Solomon – Sg

Isaiah – Is
Jeremiah – Jr
Lamentations – Lm
Ezekiel – Ezk
Daniel – Dn
Hosea – Hs
Joel – Jl
Amos – Am
Obadiah – Ob
Jonah – Jnh
Micah – Mc
Nahum – Nah
Habakkuk – Hab
Zephaniah – Zph
Haggai – Hg
Zechariah – Zch
Malachi – Mal

NEW TESTAMENT

Matthew – Mt
Mark – Mk
Luke – Lk
John – Jn

Acts – Ac
Romans – Rm
1 Corinthians – 1Co
2 Corinthians – 2Co
Galatians – Gl
Ephesians – Eph
Philippians – Php
Colossians – Col
1 Thessalonians – 1Th
2 Thessalonians – 2Th
1 Timothy – 1Tm
2 Timothy – 2Tm
Titus – Ti
Philemon – Phm
Hebrews – Heb
James – Jms
1 Peter – 1Pt
2 Peter – 2Pt
1 John – 1Jn
2 John – 2Jn
3 John – 3Jn
Jude – Jd
Revelation – Rv

Read more of Paul's letters!

Did you know we offer over fifty different Study Books to help equip you in your journey to be a woman in the Word of God every day? Our shop is filled with resources created to help you stay in Scripture.

If you enjoyed this study on Ephesians, consider one of our other Study Books on Paul's letters, like Philippians or Galatians. These letters explore what it looks like to trust in God and how to find joy in the darkest trials.

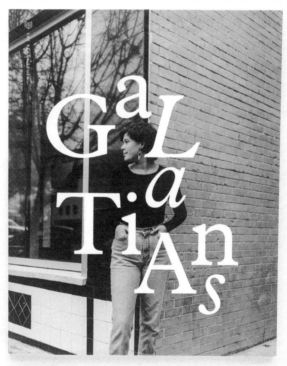

Like everything we do at She Reads
Truth, our podcast supports one simple
but powerful mission: women in the
Word of God every day.

Join us in a weekly conversation with our founders, Raechel and Amanda, as they explore
the beauty, goodness, and truth of Scripture. The She Reads Truth podcast was created as
a companion resource to the She Reads Truth reading plans, Study Books, and devotionals.
We hope this resource enhances your time in the Word!

SHE READS TRUTH
PODCAST

Love Letters & Light in the Darkness
She Reads Truth Podcast — Apr 13, 20

1×

**JOIN US ON APPLE PODCASTS OR YOUR
PREFERRED STREAMING PLATFORM.**

WHERE DID I STUDY?

O HOME
O OFFICE
O COFFEE SHOP
O CHURCH
O A FRIEND'S HOUSE
O OTHER:

WHAT WAS I LISTENING TO?

ARTIST:

SONG:

PLAYLIST:

WHEN DID I STUDY?

MORNING

AFTERNOON

NIGHT

How did I find delight in God's Word?

WHAT WAS HAPPENING IN MY LIFE?

WHAT WAS HAPPENING IN THE WORLD?

MONTH	DAY	YEAR

END DATE